Surfin' the Waves of Life ...

Always remember:

*Don't fight the Waves
— Dance with them !*

Jay Joyful

MAMBO POA

SURFIN' THE WAVES OF LIFE

A CONTEMPLATIVE SONGBOOK

Joyful-Life.org

Bibliografische Information der Deutschen Nationalbibliothek:

Die Deutsche Nationalbibliothek verzeichnet diese Publikation in der Deutschen Nationalbibliografie; detaillierte bibliografische Daten sind im Internet über http://dnb.dnb.de abrufbar.

Die automatisierte Analyse des Werkes, um daraus Informationen insbesondere über Muster, Trends und Korrelationen gemäß §44b UrhG („Text und Data Mining") zu gewinnen, ist untersagt.

© 2024 Jay Joyful

Verlag: BoD · Books on Demand GmbH, In de Tarpen 42, 22848 Norderstedt
Druck: Libri Plureos GmbH, Friedensallee 273, 22763 Hamburg
ISBN: 978-3-7693-0530-2

Content

Jay Joyful..7

About the Album..9

Surfer's Guide..12

The Songs

Mambo Poa...16

Beach Boy Dreams..22

Feelin' Hotter In The Heat...33

Love Is Love...41

Fisherman's Story...50

Blind Men And The Elephant.....................................60

Upside Down Reality...68

Unio Mystica..74

Om Mani Padme Hum (Mantra Dub)..........................80

Extra Single: *Om Mani Padme Hum,* Let the Love and Healing come..84

Walking With The Great Spirit...................................92

Appendix

Further Reading..100

Jay Joyful

Jay Joyful is an artist on a soulful mission to uplift the world through the universal language of music. Rooted in reggae rhythms and inspired by themes of unity, harmony, and inner Peace, Jay's music invites listeners to embark on a journey of self-discovery and collective empowerment. His songs reflect a deep Love for humanity and the planet, blending poetic lyrics with soothing melodies that resonate with the heart and soul.

Jay Joyful's sound is more than just music – it's a message. His work explores themes of Love, personal growth, and the search for meaning, with a particular focus on finding Peace amid Life's challenges. Whether it's through groovy reggae beats or introspective acoustic rhythms, Jay's artistry aims to inspire people to embrace their authentic selves and spread positivity to others.

As the driving force behind tracks like *"Om Mani Padme Hum"* and "Upside Down Reality," Jay weaves together playful rhythms with spiritual insights, offering both entertainment and contemplation. His debut album, "*Mambo Poa* – Surfin' on the Waves of Life", captures his philosophy of riding Life's ups and downs with grace, humour, and joy.

Jay Joyful's music is a celebration of Life's interconnectedness, echoing his core belief that Love is the greatest power, Peace is the ultimate goal, and joy is the energy that binds them all. In every beat and lyric, Jay invites the listener to join him on a journey toward a more peaceful world, with open hearts and joyful minds.

Tanzania, October 2024

Lusungu Nkwera

Listen to Jay Joyful's music, e.g. on Spotify:

also on:

Apple Music, iTunes, Instagram/Facebook, TikTok and other ByteDance stores, YouTube Music, Amazon, Pandora, Deezer, Tidal, iHeartRadio, Claro Música, Saavn, Boomplay, Anghami, NetEase, Tencent, Qobuz, Joox, Kuack Media, Adaptr, Flo, MediaNet

About the Album

Get ready to ride the rhythm of Life with "*Mambo Poa* - Surfin' on the Waves of Life," my first reggae album. It will lift your spirit and set your soul free! With the easy-going yet deeply inspiring sound of reggae, this album invites you to embrace the cool vibes of "*Mambo Poa*" – a Swahili greeting meaning "What's the matter? Everything cool." – as you surf the highs and lows of Life with Joy, Love, and Peace.

Each track is a journey, taking you through uplifting beats, soulful melodies, and lyrics that celebrate the beauty of the present moment. Whether you're seeking relaxation, reflection, or a celebration of Life's many colours, this album is the perfect companion for every mood and moment.

From the shimmering waves of tropical beach Life to the deep roots of reggae tradition, "*Mambo Poa*" is your soundtrack for living in harmony with the flow of the universe. Let the warm, uplifting rhythms carry you on a musical adventure where every wave brings a new discovery, and every song invites you to dance, dream, and feel alive.

Surfin' on the Waves of Life has never felt this good.

Titles of this Album

1. **Mambo Poa** (2:52) – Starting with the title track to set the vibe, introducing listeners to the cool, easy-going energy of the album.

2. **Beach Boy Dreams** (5:00) – Flow into this track to maintain the uplifting and carefree beach atmosphere.

3. **Feelin' Hotter in the Heat** (3:02) – Keep the energy high with this vibrant, fiery song to keep you engaged in the hot moments of Life.

4. **Love Is Love** (5:43) – A smooth transition into the universal message of Love, embracing diversity and connection.

5. **Fisherman's Story** (3:39) – Shift to a more storytelling, reflective song, grounding the listener in Life's wisdom and experiences.

6. **Blind Men And The Elephant** (9:06) – Continue the storytelling theme with a philosophical twist, offering deeper contemplation.

7. **Upside Down Reality** (2:55) – Move into a track that challenges perceptions and reality, adding a slightly more introspective or surreal tone.

8. *Unio Mystica* (3:11) – Transition into the spiritual realm with this song, introducing mystical and meditative vibes.

9. *Om Mani Padme Hum* Mantra Dub (2:56) – Deepen the spiritual journey with a mantra-based, meditative dub track, inviting reflection and Peace.

10. Walking with the Great Spirit (5:45) – End the album on a powerful, transcendent note, symbolizing a journey towards unity and connection with the greater spirit of Life.

Scan this code to listen to the album on Youtube:

Surfer's Guide

When you're "surfin' the waves of Life," here are some key principles to remember:

1. Stay Present – Be in the Moment

Just like riding a wave, Life only happens in the now. Worrying about the past or future will knock you off balance. Embrace the present moment fully, whether calm or chaotic.

2. Ride with Flow, Not Resistance

Waves cannot be controlled – they are to be ridden. Instead of fighting the current, align with Life's flow. Trust that each wave, whether high or low, has its purpose.

3. Be Light and Adaptable

Life's waves come in all shapes and sizes. Some are thrilling, some are challenging. Flexibility is key – shift your stance, adjust your focus, and keep moving forward.

4. Keep Your Balance – Embrace the Polarities

Ups and downs are natural rhythms of Life. Balance between joy and sorrow, excitement and stillness. Just like a surfer shifts their weight, we can stay centred by embracing both the highs and the lows.

5. Let Love Be Your Guide

Love is the anchor through every wave. When you ride with Love – for yourself, others, and Life itself – you'll navigate even the roughest waters with grace and courage.

6. Enjoy the Ride

Every wave is unique, and so is each moment in Life. Don't just survive – thrive and savour the experience. Life isn't just about reaching the shore; it's about enjoying the journey along the way.

7. When You Fall, Get Back Up

Falling off the board is part of the ride. Every fall is an opportunity to learn, grow, and try again with new wisdom. Keep your sense of humour intact and always paddle back out!

8. Trust the Ocean of Life

Just as the ocean has its tides, Life moves in cycles. Some waves bring joy, others bring lessons. Trust that everything happens as it should, and each wave brings you closer to your truth.

9. Connect with the Great Spirit

Like a surfer feels connected to the sea, remember that you are part of something greater. Stay connected to nature, spirit, and your higher self to find Peace amid Life's tides.

10. Dance with the Waves – Live in Harmony

Don't fight the waves – dance with them! Life is a rhythm, a melody, and each moment is an invitation to move in harmony with the music of existence. Embrace joy, creativity, and freedom in every wave.

"Surfin' the waves of Life isn't about avoiding challenges but learning to glide through them with joy, courage, and grace."

So, grab your metaphorical surfboard, stay centred, and ride every wave – because Life is an endless ocean of possibility!

The Songs

Mambo Poa

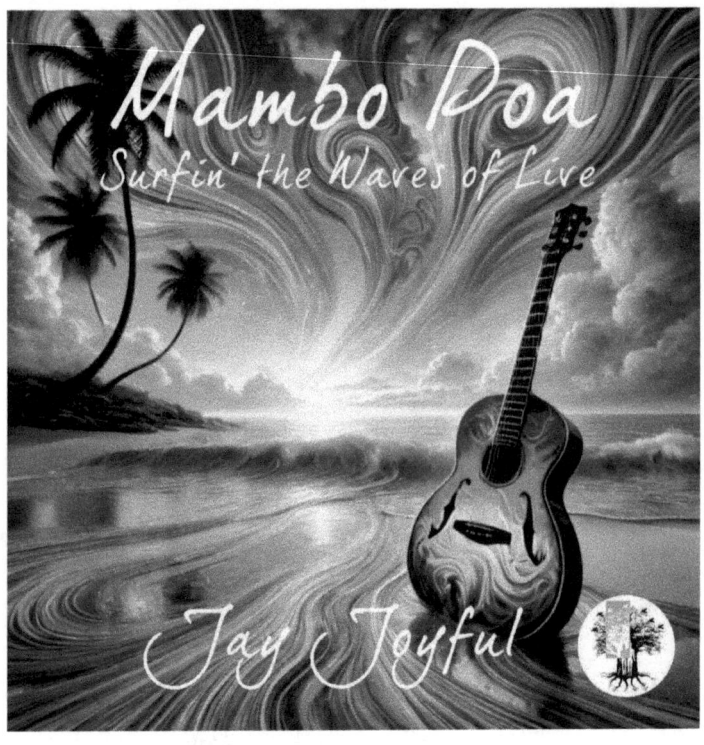

"*Mambo Poa*" is an energetic and uplifting celebration of Life, inspired by the Swahili phrase, where one askes "Mambo!?", meaning something like "How are things?" and the answer "Poa!", meaning "cool" or "things are good." The song embodies the spirit of acceptance, joy, and the ability to go with the flow – an invitation to ride the waves of Life with grace and a playful heart. Through its rhythms, it carries the essence of freedom, light-heartedness, and positivity, reminding us that Life doesn't have to be perfect for it to be beautiful.

The Flow of Life

"*Mambo Poa*" encourages us to embrace Life exactly as it is, with all its twists, turns, joys, and challenges. In Swahili, the phrase is often exchanged casually, as a way to say, "It's all cool." The song reflects this laid-back attitude, reminding us that even when things don't go according to plan, we can still find Peace by flowing with what is. It's a gentle reminder that resistance creates tension, but acceptance brings freedom.

The song invites us to ride the waves of Life like a surfer rides the ocean – finding balance, staying light, and enjoying the ride. The rhythm of "*Mambo Poa*" reflects the natural ebb and flow of Life, teaching us that joy is not something we have to chase. It's already present, waiting to be uncovered in the moments when we relax, let go, and move in harmony with the rhythm of Life.

The Art of Playfulness

At its heart, "*Mambo Poa*" celebrates playfulness – the ability to approach Life with a sense of wonder and fun. The song invites us to reconnect with that childlike energy within, reminding us that not everything has to be serious or goal-oriented. Playfulness is not just about having fun; it's about being fully present in the moment, free from worry or judgment.

Through its playful melody, the song invites us to dance, laugh, and enjoy Life's simple pleasures. It suggests that Life becomes lighter when we stop taking ourselves too seriously, and when we remember that joy is often found in the little things – a shared smile, a warm breeze, or a spontaneous dance.

A Spirit of Connection

"*Mambo Poa*" also reflects the importance of connection – with others, with nature, and with ourselves. The song encourages us to embrace community and share the good vibes. Just as the Swahili phrase is often used in conversation to spread positivity, the song calls us to radiate kindness and joy, creating ripples of connection wherever we go.

It teaches that when we meet Life with an open heart, we create space for others to do the same. "*Mambo Poa*" reminds us that happiness is contagious, and that through small acts of joy and connection, we can uplift not only ourselves but also those around us.

Living in the Present Moment

Ultimately, "*Mambo Poa*" invites us to live in the present, where Life's beauty is always unfolding. It reminds us that we don't have to wait for everything to be perfect to enjoy Life. There is joy in the now, in accepting things as they are, and in choosing to see the good even in the midst of uncertainty.

The song teaches that Peace comes not from controlling Life's outcomes but from embracing Life's rhythms. It asks us to trust the flow, to let go of unnecessary worries, and to recognize that, no matter what happens, *mambo poa* – evrything's cool. Through this attitude, we learn to surf the waves of Life with grace and gratitude, knowing that every moment is an opportunity to feel alive.

With its infectious rhythm and positive message, "*Mambo Poa*" becomes more than a song – it's a way of living, a reminder that Life's magic lies not in perfection but in presence, and that joy can always be found when we ride the waves with an open heart.

The Lyrics

[Intro]
Mambo, mambo, what's up my friend?
Poa, poa, cool vibes till the end.
We keep it chill, let the Love flow free,
Mambo poa, that's the way to be!

[Verse 1]
I wake up in the morning, sun shining bright,
Greeting my neighbour, everything feels right.
"*Mambo!*" I say with a smile so wide,
"*Poa!*" they reply, it's all good inside.
No rush, no stress, we live in the flow,
In this world of Peace, we let it grow.

[Chorus]
Mambo, mambo, what's up with you?
Poa, poa, everything's cool and true.
Mambo, mambo, let the good vibes roll,
Poa, poa, reggae rhythm in the soul.

[Verse 2]
Down by the ocean, the breeze so sweet,
Dancing to the riddim, Life's a steady beat.
"Mambo!" I shout to the ones I see,
"Poa!" they reply, we feel so free.
From the hills to the city, one thing we know,
With every *"Mambo poa,"* the Love will show.

[Chorus]
Mambo, mambo, what's up with you?
Poa, poa, everything's cool and true.
Mambo, mambo, let the good vibes roll,
Poa, poa, reggae rhythm in the soul.

[Bridge]
No matter where we go, no matter where we roam,
"Mambo poa" is the language of home.
In the heart of the people, the spirit is high,
With every word, we touch the sky.

[Chorus]
Mambo, mambo, what's up with you?
Poa, poa, everything's cool and true.
Mambo, mambo, let the good vibes roll,
Poa, poa, reggae rhythm in the soul.

[Outro]
Mambo, mambo, we greet with a smile,
Poa, poa, it's the reggae style.
Keep it light, keep it free,
Mambo poa, just you and me.

Beach Boy Dreams

The Story behind the Song

"Beach Boy Dreams" was born from a spontaneous reflection on the lives of beach boys – young men living along tropical shores, often seen as lazy, carefree, and adventurous but also misunderstood and judged. Beach boys have become part of the landscape in many vacation destinations, known for their charm, athleticism, and connection to the ocean, but also for their impertinent intrusiveness, their eagerness to somehow earn money or make a living without working themselves, and their often-played charm and seduction skills. They offer surfing lessons, boat rides, or companionship, sometimes forming romantic relationships with tourists. But beneath the surface of these interactions lies a complex and often painful reality.

Attraction and Stereotypes

Beach boys are frequently romanticized as carefree spirits – symbols of freedom and sun-kissed pleasure. Many tourists fall in Love with their charm and vitality, enchanted by the dream of fleeting romance under the sun. However, these encounters are often short-lived, leaving the beach boys to navigate a revolving door of intense but temporary connections. Sometimes, tourists feel disappointed, betrayed, or even exploited when the relationship does not meet their expectations, and accusations of manipulation, theft, or dishonesty often follow.

On the other hand, beach boys themselves face constant disrespect and judgment. They are stereotyped as hustlers or opportunists, living only to seduce tourists or take advantage of visitors. This narrow view overlooks the human behind the beach boy persona – a person with dreams, hopes, and emotions, just like anyone else. These young men, while appearing carefree, often face poverty, instability, and a lack of opportunity, trying to make a Life in a world that offers them few options.

The Heart of the Song

"Beach Boy Dreams" tells a different story – one that humanizes the beach boys and acknowledges their dreams and vulnerabilities. The song shifts the focus from the stereotypes to the inner Life of these young men, revealing that behind their bright smiles and easy charm are souls yearning for something deeper: connection, purpose, and dignity. It captures the reality that their lives are not just about fleeting moments of fun or romance but about trying to build something meaningful in a world that often leaves them stranded.

The song portrays the emotional toll of constantly forming connections that end abruptly, of giving pieces of their hearts to strangers who are gone with the next tide. These beach boys, too, dream of Love that lasts, of stability, of being seen not as an object of desire or suspicion but as human beings with real emotions. The song reflects the pain of having dreams that are repeatedly broken and desires that are dismissed as shallow or self-serving.

Empathy and Recognition

"Beach Boy Dreams" calls listeners to see beyond appearances and embrace empathy. It reminds us that the beach boys, like everyone else, are shaped by their experiences, environment, and the opportunities – or lack thereof – presented to them. Their smiles may mask disappointment, their carefree personas may hide pain, and beneath the surface, they carry dreams as valid and worthy as anyone's.

The song offers a space for those beach boys to express their longings and frustrations – a story that acknowledges not just their charm but also their humanity. It invites listeners to recognize that these young men are more than entertainment for tourists or subjects of gossip. They are individuals with their own hopes, aspirations, and struggles, trying to find meaning and Love in a transient world that often leaves them behind.

"Beach Boy Dreams" is ultimately a song of compassion – a reminder that everyone, regardless of their role or appearance, carries within them a story worth hearing. It asks us to listen, to see beyond the stereotypes, and to honour the dreams that each person carries, even when those dreams are hidden behind a playful smile and a tan. Through its melody and lyrics, the song paints a picture not just of sun and sand but of hearts searching for belonging, Love, and respect.

Contemplation about the Song

"Beach Boy Dreams" is a sunlit celebration of Life's simplicity, freedom, and the endless possibilities that arise when we let go of stress and reconnect with the playful spirit within. The song transports us to a carefree world of waves, sand, and surf – where worries are washed away by the tides, and the rhythm of the ocean becomes the rhythm of the heart. It invites us to dream, to embrace joy, and to live fully in the present, guided by the spirit of adventure and spontaneity.

A Song of Freedom and Lightness

The essence of "Beach Boy Dreams" lies in its message of freedom – the kind that comes not from escaping Life, but from embracing it with a light heart. It teaches us to step away from the busyness of daily Life and reconnect with the pure joy of simply being. Whether it's feeling the sun on our skin, the sand between our toes, or the splash of the sea against our bodies, the song reminds us that happiness is found in the small, fleeting moments when we let go and surrender to Life's natural flow.

It's a call to dance through Life with open arms, to dive into experiences without fear, and to cultivate a sense of lightness even in the face of challenges. "Beach Boy Dreams" suggests that Life, like the ocean, is best enjoyed when we ride the waves rather than resist them, flowing with its ups and downs and savouring every moment.

The Power of Play and Imagination

At its core, the song taps into the power of play and imagination – two forces that often fade as we grow older. It reminds us that within each of us lives a dreamer, someone who longs for adventure, exploration, and wonder. "Beach Boy Dreams" encourages us to rekindle that playful energy, to dream without limitations, and to create a Life that feels as vibrant and alive as a day at the beach.

This spirit of play teaches us something essential: that Life doesn't always need to be serious or planned. There is beauty in improvisation, joy in spontaneity, and magic in simply letting go and seeing where the waves take us. In this way, the song is not just about dreaming – it's about living the dream, here and now.

Connection with Nature and the Self

"Beach Boy Dreams" also reflects the deep connection between the ocean and the soul. Just as the beach offers a space of calm and renewal, the song invites us to find that same Peace within ourselves. The ocean becomes a metaphor for the inner world – vast, mysterious, and full of hidden treasures waiting to be discovered. As we immerse ourselves in its rhythms, we reconnect with the natural flow of Life, rediscovering our authentic selves beneath the noise of the outside world.

The beach represents a place where we can strip away pretence and expectations, returning to a simpler, more authentic way of being. The song gently reminds us that we don't need to travel far to find this place of Peace – it exists within us, waiting to be uncovered whenever we pause, breathe, and listen to the rhythm of our hearts.

Dreaming as a Way of Living

"Beach Boy Dreams" teaches us that dreaming is not just a nighttime activity but a way of Life. It calls us to dream boldly, not just about what we want to do but about who we want to become. Dreams, like the ocean's waves, come and go, but each one carries the potential to move us, inspire us, and shape our journey.

The song invites us to live with an open heart, embracing the beauty of the present while dreaming of new horizons. It tells us that the magic of Life lies in balancing these two states – being rooted in the now while reaching toward the future, riding the waves of reality while letting the winds of dreams carry us forward.

Ultimately, "Beach Boy Dreams" is a joyful reminder to let go, play, and live with a sense of wonder. It asks us to keep dreaming, to stay connected to our playful spirit, and to trust that Life, like the ocean, will always carry us toward new adventures if we dare to ride its waves with an open heart.

The Lyrics

[Intro]
(Yeah, yeah, yeah, yeah)
Beach boy on the shore
Dreams in my pocket, heart full of more
Watch the waves roll, watch the people go
But there's a deeper story, only few will know

[Verse 1]
I got sand in my hair and a smile on my face
Living by the ocean, I know my place
But sometimes it's lonely, yeah, I can't lie
They come for a moment, then they say goodbye

She said she loved me, called me her king
I showed her my heart, but she wanted a fling
Took her on a boat, showed her the reef
But all she wanted was a quick relief

[Chorus]
I'm just a beach boy, living in the sun
I dance with the waves, but Love's on the run
She came for a week, then she's gone in the blue
But I got my dreams, and I'm singing for you
Oh oh, yeah, yeah, singing for you
But I got my dreams, and I'm singing for you

[Verse 2]
She asked me to dance, under the stars
Promised me more, took me to the bars

But when the sun rose, she was gone like the breeze
Left me with a kiss and some stories to tease

And I ain't mad, no, I play it cool
But deep in my soul, I feel like a fool
'Cause I give them my rhythm, my fire, my sound
But when they leave, I'm back on the ground

[Bridge]
But Life's too short to cry, my friend
I'll ride these waves until the end
With laughter and Love, I carry the flame
Beach boy forever, remember my name

(Yeah, yeah, yeah, oh)

[Chorus]
I'm just a beach boy, living in the sun
I dance with the waves, but Love's on the run
She came for a week, then she's gone in the blue
But I got my dreams, and I'm singing for you
Oh oh, yeah, yeah, singing for you
But I got my dreams, and I'm singing for you

[Breakdown]
You see me smiling, but you don't know the pain
They come and go, like a summer rain
But I won't give up, I'll keep my groove
I got the rhythm, I got the moves

I want more than moments, I want something real

But these girls, they don't see how I feel
So I keep it light, I keep it bright
But deep inside, I want Love in the night

[Verse 3]
Another day, another flight
Another promise that fades with the night

But I'm still here, I'm holding on
Waiting for the one who'll sing my song

And yeah, I'll keep smiling, keep the vibe high
Even though my heart sometimes wants to cry
I'm just a beach boy, what can I say?
I'll Love the ocean, till I find my way

[Chorus]
I'm just a beach boy, living in the sun
I dance with the waves, but Love's on the run
She came for a week, then she's gone in the blue
But I got my dreams, and I'm singing for you
Oh oh, yeah, yeah, singing for you
But I got my dreams, and I'm singing for you

[Outro]
So if you see me on the sand
With a guitar and a drink in hand
Know that I'm a dreamer, playing my part
Beach boy with a reggae heart

(Oh, oh, yeah, yeah)

I'll find my queen, I'll find my Love
Until then, I'll dance with the stars above
Beach boy forever, beach boy strong
And I'll keep singing this happy song
(Yeah, yeah, yeah, oh)

Beach boy forever, beach boy strong!

Feelin' Hotter In The Heat

The song tells the story of someone who, while sweating in the tropical heat, also feels the fire of passion and desire. Instead of fighting these feelings, the desire to dive right into them prevails – into the heat, together with a hot, desirable person, and then "cool down" together.

The Story behind the Song

The inspiration for "*Feelin' Hotter in the Heat*" came from a sweltering tropical afternoon – a moment when the heat seemed to strip everything down to its raw essence. It was one of those days where the air feels thick, sweat clings to the skin, and every movement feels slow and deliberate. But with that intensity came a heightened sense of awareness – of the body, of sensations, of desires stirring just beneath the surface.

It was during this time that the idea for the song emerged: *What if, instead of resisting the heat – both physical and emotional – we leaned into it?* The heat became a metaphor for the powerful pull of passion, attraction, and desire. Much like the tropical sun, these feelings can be overwhelming, yet they carry the promise of something exhilarating if we surrender to them.

A Chance Encounter in the Heat

The heart of the story is rooted in an encounter – a spark between two people under the sun's relentless blaze. The setting was perfect: a tropical paradise, with ocean waves glimmering nearby and the air buzzing with possibility. The connection was undeniable, the chemistry palpable, like two flames drawn together, feeding off the heat of the moment.

Rather than fighting the intensity, both individuals gave in to it, allowing the fire of attraction to burn bright. They let go of inhibitions and embraced the heat – not only of the weather but of the emotions stirring within them. The song captures this experience: the joy of surrendering to desire, the thrill of being fully alive in the moment, and the playfulness of finding someone who is willing to dive into that intensity with you.

Cooling Down Together

The song also hints at the sweetness that follows – after the fire of passion comes the cool, refreshing relief, like a breeze blowing through after the hottest part of the day. The heat doesn't last forever, but what remains is a feeling of connection, satisfaction, and lightness. The lyrics capture both the build-up and the release, the heat and the cool-down, reflecting the natural rhythm of Life and Love.

"Feelin' Hotter in the Heat" ultimately tells a story of two people daring to embrace the intensity of the moment – without fear or hesitation. It's about the courage to lean into Life's fiery moments, knowing that on the other side of passion lies a sense of freedom and joy. The song celebrates those fleeting, electric connections that leave us breathless, reminding us that sometimes the best way to deal with the heat is to dive right in and enjoy the ride.

Contemplation about the Song

"Feelin' Hotter in the Heat" captures the intensity, passion, and wild energy that arise when we embrace Life's fire – those moments when everything feels heightened, alive, and electric. The song plays with the metaphor of heat, not just as physical warmth but as the inner flame that drives desire, creativity, and transformation. It reminds us that, like the scorching sun, Life can be both invigorating and overwhelming, pushing us beyond comfort zones and calling us to dance with the fire rather than hide from it.

The Fire of Passion and Desire

At the heart of "Feelin' Hotter in the Heat" lies the celebration of passion – the raw, untamed force that fuels Love, art, and adventure. It reflects those moments when desire ignites, leaving us breathless and alive, as if every sensation is intensified by the heat. The song encourages us to welcome these fiery emotions, recognizing them as catalysts for growth and transformation. Passion, whether it burns in romance, creativity, or personal ambition, is the energy that moves us forward, breaking through stagnation and awakening new possibilities.

The song suggests that feeling the heat – whether emotional, physical, or spiritual – is part of what it means to be fully alive. It teaches us not to fear intensity but to embrace it, knowing that fire has the power to purify, awaken, and illuminate the path ahead.

The Challenge of Staying Present

"Feelin' Hotter in the Heat" also speaks to the challenge of staying present when Life gets intense. Just as heat can be both exhilarating and exhausting, so too can the pressures and passions of Life. The song invites us to remain grounded even when everything around us feels heightened, to dance with Life's intensity rather than be consumed by it.

This message is a reminder that, like summer's heat, Life's intensity comes in waves. Some moments will burn with excitement and inspiration, while others will feel overwhelming or draining. The key is to stay present – to ride the heat without retreating, trusting that every fiery moment will eventually give way to cool breezes and calm.

Transformation through Heat

The song also touches on heat as a force of transformation. Just as fire reshapes everything it touches, the heat of Life's challenges can change us, revealing strengths and truths we didn't know we had. It teaches us that transformation isn't always easy or comfortable – sometimes it means being thrown into the fire, stripped of old patterns, and forged into something new.

"Feelin' Hotter in the Heat" encourages us to welcome these transformative moments, knowing that they are part of our evolution. The discomfort that heat brings is often the very thing that leads to breakthroughs, awakening us to new dimensions of ourselves.

The Rhythm of Life's Seasons

The song also reflects the rhythm of Life's seasons – how every phase, even the fiery ones, has its purpose. Just as summer's heat energizes the world with growth and movement, Life's intense moments bring opportunities for expansion and adventure. The song teaches us to dance through these seasons, embracing the highs and lows, and trusting that each moment – whether hot or cool – is part of a larger rhythm.

Ultimately, "Feelin' Hotter in the Heat" is an invitation to celebrate the fire within and around us. It calls us to feel deeply, Love boldly, and live passionately, knowing that heat is both a gift and a challenge. By embracing Life's fiery moments with an open heart, we allow ourselves to burn brightly, illuminating the path ahead and awakening to the fullness of who we are.

The Lyrics

[Verse 1]
The sun is blazin', burnin' up the sky,
I wipe my brow, as the sweat rolls by.
The heat's so strong, can't take no more,
Then you walk by, and my temperature soars.

Oh, you're hotter than this midday sun,
Got me feelin' like I'm the only one.
I'm thirsty now, but not for a drink,
I'm thinkin' 'bout you, baby, make me blink!

[Chorus]
Feelin' hot, so hot, yeah, I can't cool down,
Your fire got me spinnin' 'round and 'round.
In this heat, let's go with the flow,
Whatever happens, let's take it slow.
Feelin' hot, so hot, from head to toe,
You're burnin' me up, and I'm ready to go!

[Verse 2]
This summer heat ain't got nothin' on you,
You're hotter than a flame, yeah, that's true.
I see you movin', swayin' in the breeze,
Baby, come closer, won't you please?

I'm meltin' down, like ice on the street,
You got that fire that's impossible to beat.
I don't need no fan, don't need no shade,
Just you and me, let the heat invade.

[Chorus]
Feelin' hot, so hot, yeah, I can't cool down,
Your fire got me spinnin' 'round and 'round.
In this heat, let's go with the flow,
Whatever happens, let's take it slow.
Feelin' hot, so hot, from head to toe,
You're burnin' me up, and I'm ready to go!

[Bridge]
The temperature's risin', I can't deny,
But I don't mind if we let sparks fly.
No need to rush, no need to fight,
Just you and me, let's burn through the night.

Oh baby, the heat is more than I can bear,
But with you here, I really don't care.
Let the sun blaze on, let the sweat pour,
You got me wantin' more and more!

[Chorus]
Feelin' hot, so hot, yeah, I can't cool down,
Your fire got me spinnin' 'round and 'round.
In this heat, let's go with the flow,
Whatever happens, let's take it slow.
Feelin' hot, so hot, from head to toe,
You're burnin' me up, and I'm ready to go!

[Outro]
The heat is wild, but you're wilder still,
And baby, I'm down for that thrill.
Let's let it ride, let's let it be,
In this heat, it's just you and me.

Feelin' hot, so hot, don't wanna stop,
In this fire, let's let it pop!
Feelin' hotter, hotter, don't need no breeze,
Come close, baby, and cool me please!

Love Is Love

"Love is Love" is a celebration of the pure, universal nature of Love – a force that transcends boundaries, definitions, and limitations. At its core, the song reminds us that Love is not confined by labels or categories. It is not bound by gender, race, status, or circumstance. Love is simply Love – an energy that flows freely, connecting hearts and souls in ways that defy the logic of the mind.

The song reflects the truth that Love is inherent to Life itself. It is the essence that unites all beings, the force that brings us closer to each other and to our true selves. Love is not something that needs to be earned or justified – it simply is. Whether it manifests between lovers, friends, family, or even strangers, Love is Love in all its forms, equally sacred and meaningful.

Eros without Limitations or Judgements

"Love is Love" also celebrates erotic Love as a sacred and liberating force, transcending societal norms, taboos, or moral constructs. It reminds us that erotic Love – the deep, sensual connection between two souls – exists beyond the rules imposed by culture or convention. This kind of Love is not merely physical; it is an ecstatic merging of bodies, minds, and spirits, where desire becomes a gateway to transcendence. When expressed with mutual respect, presence, and authenticity, erotic Love invites us to shed shame and guilt, reclaiming our innate right to experience pleasure and intimacy. The song encourages us to honour these connections in their purest form, recognizing that Love, in all its expressions, is a divine force. By embracing erotic Love without judgment, we expand our capacity to experience wholeness, freedom, and unity, dissolving the false boundaries between the spiritual and the sensual.

The Universality of Love

In a world that often seeks to divide and categorize, "Love is Love" calls us to remember the unity that lies beneath the surface of our differences. Love does not recognize the barriers we create – it flows where it is needed, healing wounds, bridging gaps, and dissolving separation.

The song emphasizes that Love is a universal language. It doesn't require translation or explanation. Whether expressed through a warm embrace, a kind word, or a silent presence, Love communicates directly from heart to heart. It teaches us to see beyond appearances and connect with the essence of another being, recognizing that we are all part of the same dance of Life.

Love as an Act of Courage

"Love is Love" also reflects the courage it takes to Love fully and openly. In a world where fear, prejudice, and misunderstanding can often cloud our hearts, to Love without conditions or restrictions is a radical act. The song encourages us to move beyond fear – to embrace the vulnerability of loving and being loved.

It reminds us that Love is not always easy; it asks us to be patient, forgiving, and open even in challenging times. But through these acts of Love, we discover our deepest strength. The song teaches that Love is not a finite resource to be measured or withheld – it is boundless, expanding as we give it freely.

The Healing Power of Love

"Love is Love" is also a song of healing. It speaks to the ability of Love to mend what is broken, to soften what is hardened, and to bring light to places of darkness. The song encourages us to Love ourselves as we are, to embrace our imperfections, and to recognize that we are worthy of Love simply because we exist.

In loving ourselves and others, we participate in the healing of the world. The song reminds us that every act of Love – no matter how small – has the power to transform, ripple outward, and touch lives in ways we may never fully see. Love is the thread that weaves us together, reminding us that we are never truly alone.

Living the Truth of "Love is Love"

To live the truth of "Love is Love" is to embody Love in all that we do. It means showing up with kindness, compassion, and presence, even in the face of misunderstanding or opposition. It means celebrating Love in all its forms, honouring the diversity of relationships and expressions that make Life beautiful.

The song teaches us that Love is not confined to romantic relationships – it is found in every connection, every moment of care, and every act of service. It asks us to recognize the divine in every encounter and to live with the awareness that Love is both the path and the destination.

Love as a Sacred Force

Ultimately, "Love is Love" reminds us that Love is sacred. It is the energy that flows through the universe, the essence that sustains Life, and the force that guides us home to ourselves and each other. In loving, we align ourselves with the most powerful truth of all: that we are all connected, that we are all worthy, and that Love is the essence of everything.

Through this song, we are invited to live boldly, to love without fear, and to embrace the beauty of being fully alive. It calls us to open our hearts wide, to dissolve the walls that separate us, and to remember that no matter who or where we are, Love is Love – and it is always enough.

The Lyrics

[Verse 1]
Love is Love, that's how it flows,
In every heart, it grows and grows,
We're all the same, no need to divide,
Love brings us together, side by side.
It's not who you Love, but how you care,
The way you give, the way you share,
Every bit of Love makes the world bright,
Healing our souls, shining the light.

[Chorus]
Love is Love, let it shine, let it flow,
In every heart, let it grow and glow,
No walls, no chains, no rules to bind,
Just Love pure and true, of every kind.
Love is Love, it's all we need to be,
Set your heart free, let it be unity,
Every bit of Love makes the world a better place,
And brings us Peace in Life's embrace.

[Verse 2]
It doesn't matter who, it's all about the heart,
Love is the bond that never falls apart,
It's the rhythm of Life, the song of the soul,
The warmth of connection that makes us whole.
It's how you Love that lights the way,
Let it grow stronger with each passing day,
Open your heart, let Love take flight,
It's the only way we shine so bright.

[Chorus]
Love is Love, let it shine, let it flow,
In every heart, let it grow and glow,
No walls, no chains, no rules to bind,
Just Love pure and true, of every kind.
Love is Love, it's all we need to be,
Set your heart free, let it be unity,
Every bit of Love makes the world a better place,
And brings us Peace in Life's embrace.

[Verse 3]
Love one, Love two, Love three or four,
Open your heart, let it Love even more,
No limits, no fear, just let it be,
Love in all forms, sets the spirit free.
It's not the number, it's the feeling inside,
Love is the truth, with nothing to hide,
Whether many or few, it's all the same,
Love is Love, no need for shame.

[Chorus]
Love is Love, let it shine, let it flow,
In every heart, let it grow and glow,
No walls, no chains, no rules to bind,
Just Love pure and true, of every kind.
Love is Love, it's all we need to be,
Set your heart free, let it be unity,
Every bit of Love makes the world a better place,
And brings us Peace in Life's embrace.

[Verse 4]
Love him or her, or it or them,
Love knows no borders, it's all the same,
No matter the face, no matter the name,
In every heart, Love burns the flame.
Love is a force, it knows no bounds,
It lifts us up, turns us around,
From every corner, from near or far,
Love is the light, the shining star.

[Chorus]
Love is Love, let it shine, let it flow,
In every heart, let it grow and glow,
No walls, no chains, no rules to bind,
Just Love pure and true, of every kind.
Love is Love, it's all we need to be,
Set your heart free, let it be unity,
Every bit of Love makes the world a better place,
And brings us Peace in Life's embrace.

[instrumental interlude]

Love is Love, and that's the way it goes,
In the heart it grows, no matter what you chose,
human ist human, we all are the same,
No need to point fingers, no need for shame.
It's not who you Love, but how you give,
The way your heart opens, the way you live,
Every bit of Love makes this world whole,
Healing all wounds, deep in the soul.

[Chorus]
Love is Love, let it shine, let it flow,
In every heart, let it grow and glow,
No walls, no chains, no rules to bind,
Just Love pure and true, of every kind.
Love is Love, it's all we need to be,
Set your heart free, let it be unity,
Every bit of Love makes the world a better place,
And brings us Peace in Life's embrace.
[Bridge]

Feel the Love in the breeze, let it carry you high,
With every heartbeat, feel the reason why,
From the mountains high to the rivers deep,
Love is the bond that we must keep.
It's about the way you Love, the way you show,
In Love we rise, in Love we grow,
No need to fight, no need to hide,
In Love we're free, in Love we're alive.

[Chorus]
Love is Love, let it shine, let it flow,
In every heart, let it grow and glow,
No walls, no chains, no rules to bind,
Just Love pure and true, of every kind.
Love is Love, it's all we need to be,
Set your heart free, let it be unity,
Every bit of Love makes the world a better place,
And brings us Peace in Life's embrace.

[Outro]
So let Love be Love, let it rise and shine,
In every colour, in every line,
From the depths of the heart, to the stars above,
We are one, we are Love, yeah, Love is Love.

Fisherman's Story

The Story behind the Song

One day, a wealthy businessman was vacationing in a small coastal village. As he walked along the pier, he noticed a fisherman pulling in a modest catch of fish early in the morning. Curious, the businessman approached and struck up a conversation.

Businessman: "That's a fine catch you have there. How long did it take you to catch these fish?"

Fisherman: "Not too long, maybe a couple of hours."

Businessman (startled by the fact that the fisherman is sitting under the mango tree in daytime instead of working): "Why didn't you stay out longer to catch more fish?"

The fisherman smiled, his weathered face peaceful under the morning sun.

Fisherman: "This is enough for my family. We'll have food for the day, and I can sell a few fish to buy what else we need."

Intrigued, the businessman leaned in, thinking he could share some wisdom.

Businessman: "But if you stayed out longer and caught more fish, you could sell them, make more money, and maybe buy a bigger boat."

Fisherman: "And then what?"

Businessman: "Well, with a bigger boat, you could catch even more fish and start earning enough to buy a fleet of boats. You could hire people to fish for you, and soon you could build your own fishing company."

The fisherman looked at him patiently, tilting his head slightly.

Fisherman: "And then?"

The businessman, excited by the vision, explained further: "With your company growing, you could move to the city, manage operations, and expand internationally. You'd become very wealthy."

The fisherman gave a small nod, as if considering the idea, and asked once more:

Fisherman: "And then?"

"Then," said the businessman with a grin, "you could retire, move to a small coastal village, fish in the mornings, spend time with your family, and enjoy Life."

The fisherman smiled again, this time with a knowing look.

Fisherman: "But that's what I'm already doing."

The Moral of the Story

This story gently points to the idea that true wealth is not found in endless striving but in the simplicity of being content with what you have. The fisherman's wisdom reflects the truth that Peace, happiness, and fulfilment are available in the present moment, not just in some distant future goal.

The businessman's view of success reflects the common belief that happiness lies in achieving more, acquiring wealth, or working harder to build a dream Life. But the fisherman sees through the illusion. He has already found contentment in a Life filled with purpose, Love, and connection – without the need for external validation or more possessions.

This story is a reminder that Life is not a race to accumulate but a journey to be enjoyed. It challenges us to ask ourselves: Are we chasing after something we already have? Are we postponing our happiness for a future that may never come, while the beauty of Life is already unfolding right in front of us?

In the end, it invites us to pause, breathe, and reconsider what it means to live a rich Life.

Contemplation about the song

"Fisherman's Story" is a poetic journey that takes us to the heart of a simple yet profound truth about Life. Through the metaphor of a fisherman casting his net into the unknown depths of the sea, the song explores themes of faith, patience, surrender, and trust in the rhythms of Life. Like a fisherman waiting for the tides to bring their gifts, the song invites us to embrace Life's uncertainties and to trust that, in time, everything we need will come to us.

The Sea as a Symbol of the Unknown

The sea in "Fisherman's Story" represents the vast, mysterious flow of existence – the deep unknown that cannot be controlled or fully understood. It reminds us that Life does not operate on our schedules or expectations. The fisherman, like each of us, casts his net with hope, yet has no guarantee of what it will catch. Some days, the sea may offer an abundance of fish, while other days, the net may return empty. This mirrors the ebb and flow of our own lives – moments of fulfilment followed by periods of longing or stillness.

The song teaches that to live well, we must learn to embrace both the fullness and the emptiness. It is in surrendering to the unknown – trusting the rhythms of the sea – that we discover Peace. Just as the fisherman knows that patience is part of the craft, we are reminded to cultivate trust in the timing of Life, knowing that each moment holds value, whether it brings abundance or stillness.

The Net as a Metaphor for Effort and Surrender

In "Fisherman's Story," the act of casting the net becomes a metaphor for the balance between effort and surrender. The fisherman cannot simply wait on the shore; he must venture into the waters and throw his net, trusting that the sea will respond. The song reflects the wisdom of balancing action with acceptance – doing our part with dedication and intention, while releasing the need to control the outcome.

This balance is essential to a meaningful Life. We cast our nets in many ways – through Love, creativity, work, and relationships – hoping to gather meaning, joy, and connection. But not everything we seek will come to us immediately, nor will every effort yield results. The song encourages us to let go of rigid expectations, to trust that what is meant for us will arrive, and to remain open to unexpected blessings.

Patience and Presence

The Life of a fisherman is one of waiting – watching the tides, reading the currents, and knowing when to cast the net. This waiting is not passive but filled with presence and awareness. "Fisherman's Story" invites us to cultivate a similar patience in our own Lives. It reminds us that rushing through Life or forcing outcomes only creates tension. Instead, we are called to be fully present in each moment, trusting that Life's gifts will arrive when the time is right.

The song teaches that every moment of waiting is sacred, a chance to deepen our relationship with ourselves, with others, and with Life itself. The fisherman's patience mirrors the practice of mindfulness – being here, now, with an open heart, whether the net is full or empty.

Gratitude for the Catch and the Journey

At its heart, "Fisherman's Story" is a song of gratitude – for the journey, the lessons, and the gifts that come, whether expected or not. It reminds us that the true treasure is not only in what we catch but in the act of casting the net, in the courage to venture into the unknown, and in the grace to accept whatever Life brings. The song teaches us to appreciate the journey itself, recognizing that every step, every experience, and every moment of waiting has its purpose.

Whether the net is filled with fish or returns empty, the fisherman's heart is one of gratitude. The song invites us to adopt the same attitude in our lives – to be thankful for both the joys and the challenges, knowing that each has something to teach us.

Life as a Sacred Fishing Expedition

Ultimately, "Fisherman's Story" reminds us that Life itself is a sacred fishing expedition. We are all fishermen, casting our nets into the great sea of existence, gathering experiences, insights, and connections along the way. Some days bring abundance, while others bring emptiness – but both are essential parts of the journey. The song teaches us to walk through Life with an open heart, a patient spirit, and a deep trust in the unseen currents that guide us.

In the end, "Fisherman's Story" is not just about fishing; it is about Life, Love, and the art of letting go. It invites us to trust the journey, to cast our nets with faith, and to find Peace in the knowledge that everything we need will come – perhaps not when or how we expect, but in perfect time, like the tides returning to the shore.

The Lyrics

[Intro]
Yeah, let me tell you my story,
Livin' Life simple, feelin' glory.
I'm a fisherman, and this is my song,
I know what I need, I don't need to chase for long …

[Verse 1]
I sit beneath the shady tree, by the ocean blue,
Caught my fish, now I'm through.
The sun is warm, the breeze is kind,
I've found my Peace, I've cleared my mind.

Then came a man in a fancy suit,
Asked me why I don't pursue more loot.
He said, "You could work, you could strive,
Build yourself a big empire and thrive."

[Pre-Chorus]
But I just smiled, said, "I'm fine,
I've got enough, I've got my time.
What more could I really need?
Life's about Peace, not endless greed."

[Chorus]
Why should I rush, why should I run?
When my day's work is already done.
I could chase the gold, the fame, the high,
But my real treasure's in the clear blue sky.
Peace and Love, that's all I need,

Not a Life of endless greed.
I take my time, enjoy the ride,
'Cause happiness is right inside.

[Verse 2]
The man, he said, "Don't you see,
You could have it all, just like me.
A bigger boat, a larger crew,
More fish, more cash, you know it's true."

But I just laughed, shook my head,
"If I did all that, I'd end up right here," I said.
"With all that wealth, and all that time,
I'd be sittin' back here watchin' Life unwind."

[Pre-Chorus]
I catch my fish, I live my day,
I Love my Life in a simple way.
I don't need more to feel complete,
I've already got the world at my feet.

[Chorus]
Why should I rush, why should I run?
When my day's work is already done.
I could chase the gold, the fame, the high,
But my real treasure's in the clear blue sky.
Peace and Love, that's all I need,
Not a Life of endless greed.
I take my time, enjoy the ride,
'Cause happiness is right inside.

[Bridge]
So, you see, my friend, I've found my place,
I don't need to join that endless race.
I've got my joy, I've got my day,
I wouldn't trade this Life away.

[instrumental interlude]

[Chorus]
Why should I rush, why should I run?
When my day's work is already done.
I could chase the gold, the fame, the high,
But my real treasure's in the clear blue sky.
Peace and Love, that's all I need,
Not a Life of endless greed.
I take my time, enjoy the ride,
'Cause happiness is right inside.

[Outro]
Yeah, I know what I got, and I know what I need,
I got the ocean, the sun, and the sea breeze.
I'm not chasin' more, I'm livin' free,
This simple Life is enough for me …

Blind Men And The Elephant

"Blind Men and the Elephant" takes us on a lyrical journey through an ancient parable, offering profound insights into the nature of perception, truth, and unity. The story of several blind men, each touching a different part of the elephant and insisting that their fragment is the whole truth, symbolizes the limitations of human understanding. The song invites us to reflect on how our personal experiences, beliefs, and perspectives shape the way we see the world – and how easily we can mistake our partial truths for the entire reality.

The Fragmented Truth

Each blind man in the story is right, but only partially so. One feels the trunk and declares the elephant to be like a snake, another touches a leg and insists it is like a tree, while another, grasping the ear, believes it resembles a fan. The song illustrates the tendency of human beings to cling to their own limited perspective, unaware that the greater truth lies beyond what we can grasp with our senses or minds.

This parable, woven into the song, becomes a reflection on how our personal narratives, ideologies, and experiences can limit us. It reminds us that no matter how certain we are of our understanding, we are only seeing part of the picture. The elephant – like Life itself – is vast and multidimensional, impossible to fully comprehend from any single point of view.

The Dance of Perspectives

The song encourages us to embrace humility and openness. In a world where people often argue over their differing perceptions, it offers a gentle reminder that truth is not something we possess but something we approach through dialogue, openness, and shared experience. Rather than clinging to our own perspective, the song invites us to dance with multiple viewpoints, recognizing that each holds a piece of the puzzle.

Through its rhythm and melody, "Blind Men and the Elephant" evokes the interplay of different perspectives. Just as the blind men's individual experiences were fragments of a greater whole, so too are the diverse beliefs, cultures, and paths of humanity. The song calls us to move beyond judgment, to listen deeply, and to honour the truths of others, even when they differ from our own.

Unity in Diversity

"Blind Men and the Elephant" also serves as a metaphor for unity in diversity. The elephant represents the interconnectedness of Life – a wholeness that can only be realized when we acknowledge the value of different perspectives. In the same way that each part of the elephant is essential to the whole, each person, belief, and experience adds to the richness of Life.

The song encourages us to move from fragmentation to unity, from division to connection. It teaches that we are not separate from one another but part of the same great body of existence, just as the trunk, legs, and ears are all part of the same elephant. In recognizing this unity, we learn to see beyond our differences and embrace the wholeness of Life.

Seeing with the Heart

Ultimately, the song suggests that true understanding comes not from the mind alone but from the heart. To walk the path of wisdom, we must go beyond what we think we know, opening ourselves to mystery, compassion, and wonder. The blind men's mistake was not that they touched the elephant but that they failed to listen to each other's experiences. The song invites us to listen not just with our ears but with our hearts, recognizing that each perspective holds a glimmer of truth.

"Blind Men and the Elephant" is more than a story – it is a mirror, reflecting the human tendency to grasp at fragments while missing the larger picture. But it also offers a way forward: by opening our minds and hearts, by honouring the perspectives of others, and by embracing the mystery of the whole, we step closer to wisdom. The song reminds us that Life's truth is not a puzzle to be solved but a dance to be experienced – a dance where every step, every encounter, and every perspective matters.

Through this contemplative journey, the song becomes an invitation: let us move through the world with humility, curiosity, and compassion, knowing that the great elephant of Life is far more beautiful and complex than any of us can see alone.

The Lyrics

[Intro]
Oh yeah, yeah, yeah …
Open your mind, yeah, see what's true …
'Cause the world we live in, it's bigger than me and you …
Come together now, let's understand …
We're all just pieces of a bigger plan…

[Chorus]
Blind men and the elephant, we're all feelin' just one part,
Tryin' to make sense of the world, but we're still in the dark.
Every man's got his truth, but no one sees the whole,
Until we learn to come together, heart to heart and soul to soul.

[Verse 1]
The first man touched the trunk, said, "The elephant's a snake!"
But he couldn't see beyond, he made a big mistake.
He felt the curve, the twist, the way it moved and swayed,
He didn't know the truth, he just saw what he had made.

The second man reached out, touched the elephant's big ear,
"It's just like a fan, there's nothin' more here."

But the elephant was vast, much bigger than he thought,
He saw just a little, but the whole he never caught.

[Chorus]
Blind men and the elephant, we're all feelin' just one part,
Tryin' to make sense of the world, but we're still in the dark.
Every man's got his truth, but no one sees the whole,
Until we learn to come together, heart to heart and soul to soul.

[Verse 2]
The third man touched the leg, said, "It's like a mighty tree!"
Firm and strong and steady, that's all the elephant could be.
But he didn't know, he couldn't see the rest,
Thought he knew the truth, but he missed the test.

The fourth one grabbed the tail, said, "It's just like a rope!"
Swung it back and forth, he lost all hope.
He didn't see the giant, didn't see the grace,
Judged by just a piece, missed the whole elephant's face.

[Bridge]
Oh, can't you see? We're all blind sometimes,
Thinkin' we know it all, but missin' the signs.

If we'd only stop, take each other's hand,
Maybe together, we'd finally understand.

[Chorus]
Blind men and the elephant, we're all feelin' just one part,
Tryin' to make sense of the world, but we're still in the dark.
Every man's got his truth, but no one sees the whole,
Until we learn to come together, heart to heart and soul to soul.

[Verse 3]
So come on now, brothers, come on now, sisters too,
We're all just blind men, searching for the truth.
Each of us with pieces, but the puzzle's never done,
Till we open up our minds, and unite as one.

[instrumental interlude]

The elephant is Life, bigger than we see,
And every single person holds a piece of destiny.
So let's lay down our pride, and listen to each other,
In this world of mystery, every man's our brother.

[Outro]
Blind men and the elephant, now we start to see,
The bigger picture's waiting, for you and for me.
We'll never know it all, but that's alright,
When we walk together, we can find the light …
yeah …

Blind men and the elephant,
we're all feelin' just one part …
Open up your heart …
and you'll see the start …

Blind men and the elephant …
oh yeah …
feelin' just one part …
Let's come together now …
and find the light …

[reprise]

Upside Down Reality

"Upside Down World" reflects the paradoxes and contradictions of Life, and especially in contemporary Life – a world where appearances deceive, where the truth is often hidden beneath illusions, and where everything seems inverted. The song explores the disorienting experience of living in a reality where what is good can appear evil, and what is wrong can masquerade as right. It invites us to question the status quo, see beyond the surface, and recognize that transformation begins when we confront the world as it is, rather than how it seems.

This song speaks to the discomfort of navigating a world that feels upside down. It challenges us to awaken from collective illusions, calling out the systems that perpetuate suffering, inequality, and division. But it also offers hope: even in a world turned on its head, there is an opportunity to find meaning, to unlearn what limits us, and to embrace a new way of being.

The Gift of Perception

The world may seem chaotic, but "Upside Down World" reminds us that the confusion we encounter can be a gateway to wisdom. It is in the disorientation that we begin to question, and in questioning, we find new truths. The song encourages us to shift our perspective, to look at Life from different angles, and to uncover the hidden harmony beneath the apparent chaos.

In an upside-down world, we are called to see with the heart, to trust intuition over appearances, and to discover deeper realities beyond what the eyes perceive. When we do, we realize that the very things that seem like obstacles – pain, loss, or confusion – can become teachers, leading us closer to inner clarity.

A Call to Reimagine the World

"Upside Down World" also carries a subtle invitation: to reimagine the world, not as it is, but as it could be. It points to the need for transformation – not only on a personal level but also collectively. This means questioning the norms that divide us, challenging the beliefs that separate us from each other and from nature, and embracing values rooted in Love, unity, and Peace.

Through the song, we are invited to embrace paradox. It asks: What if we learn to dance with uncertainty instead of fearing it? What if we see beauty in the brokenness and possibility in the mess? It teaches that there is strength in vulnerability, clarity in confusion, and freedom in letting go of rigid truths.

Living in Alignment with the Inverted Truth

In this upside-down world, we learn that the path forward is not always a straight line. The song encourages us to accept that sometimes, the way up is down, the way forward is through, and the way to Peace is surrender. When we embrace these inverted truths, we align ourselves with the natural flow of Life – a flow that transcends logic and opens us to grace.

"Upside Down World" invites us to laugh at the absurdity of Life, to cultivate lightness even in the face of darkness, and to live with open hearts in a world that often encourages closed minds. It reminds us that we are part of a cosmic play, where everything is impermanent, and nothing is exactly as it seems.

Finding Balance in the Upside Down

Ultimately, the song teaches that while the world may feel upside down, balance is always possible. We find it not by resisting the contradictions, but by embracing them. It is in the dance of opposites – light and dark, joy and sorrow, certainty and doubt – that we discover our equilibrium.

"Upside Down World" reminds us that we have the power to create meaning, even in the midst of confusion. It invites us to be conscious creators in a world where illusions abound, and to bring the truth of our hearts into every action, word, and thought. In doing so, we become the architects of a new reality, one where Love reigns and unity prevails – turning the upside-down world right-side up.

The Lyrics

[Verse 1]
Plastic flowers bloom in the desert night,
Healthy are sick, but it feels so right.
Shadows dance in the light of the fake,
Truth bends and twists until it breaks.
Boom! Clap! Logic's out of sight,
The blind can see, but we've lost the fight.
Jump the fence, reality's torn,
In a world upside down, we're forever reborn.

[Chorus]
Zig-zag minds in a twisted flow,
Truth is lost, and we don't even know.
Lies shine bright where the stars should be,
Dada dada, is this the world we see?

[Verse 2]
Giraffes play maracas in the street of lies,
Bicycles hum to the tune of disguise.
Circles fall, triangles rise,
Real is fake, but clever is the prize.
Cotton candy trees, the sick that heal,
In this crazy world, what is real?
The moon's a turtle, but the turtle's fake,
Nonsense rules, for sense's sake!

[Chorus]
Zig-zag minds in a twisted flow,
Truth is lost, and we don't even know.
Lies shine bright where the stars should be,
Dada dada, is this the world we see?

[Bridge]
War is Peace, and Peace is war,
The line between them's never been so blurred before.
Nonsense is clever, and truth's a lie,
In this world of madness, we still get by.

[Chorus]
Zig-zag minds in a twisted flow,

Truth is lost, and we don't even know.
Lies shine bright where the stars should be,
Dada dada, is this the world we see?
[instrumental interlude]

[Chorus]
Zig-zag minds in a twisted flow,
Truth is lost, and we don't even know.
Lies shine bright where the stars should be,
Dada dada, is this the world we see?

[Outro]
So let the riddim flow, let the madness reign,
In this upside world, nothing's the same.
Reggae beats in a dada dream,
Love is real, but nothing's as it seems!

[reprise]

Unio Mystica

"Unio Mystica" – the mystical union – speaks to the sacred experience of oneness with the Divine, where the boundaries between self and the universe dissolve, revealing the interconnected dance of Life. This state of union transcends the mind's dualities, harmonizing opposites: light and shadow, masculine and feminine, spirit and matter. It is the moment when the lover and the beloved become one, and all separation gives way to unity.

At its core, *"Unio Mystica"* invites us to surrender the ego, to dissolve into Love so profound that we no longer know where we end and the divine begins. It is not an escape from the world but a deep immersion into its essence, recognizing that the ordinary is infused with sacredness. Every breath becomes a prayer, every heartbeat a hymn, and every encounter with another being becomes a reflection of the divine presence within and around us.

Unio Mystica as a Dance of Polarities

The song reflects the alchemical marriage of opposites – the *yin* and *yang*, the earthly and the transcendent – merging them into a harmonious whole. This mystical dance encourages us to embrace both pleasure and pain, chaos and Peace, as parts of a greater cosmic rhythm. Just as the wave cannot be separated from the ocean, we come to understand that our individual existence is inseparably woven into the divine fabric of all Life.

"Unio Mystica" suggests that enlightenment is not found in distancing oneself from earthly experiences but in fully embracing them, seeing them as gateways to the divine. It is the realization that Love, intimacy, and deep connection with Life in all its forms – with Lovers, nature, music, and stillness – are all expressions of the same sacred unity.

The Journey to Union

To experience *Unio Mystica* is to step beyond fear and control, into trust and surrender. It asks us to let go of our need to define and grasp, to allow the river of Life to carry us toward union without resistance. The soul's journey, like the song itself, is not linear but cyclical, unfolding in spirals – moments of ecstasy, moments of emptiness, and moments where the heart breaks open, only to discover that Love is limitless.

Each verse, each note, becomes a prayer in this unfolding. The listener is invited to journey inward, to experience the divine not as a distant concept but as something intimately present, both within and without. In this mystical union, every sound, every silence becomes the voice of the Beloved, calling us home to ourselves.

The Song as a Portal

"*Unio Mystica*" is more than a song; it is a portal – an invitation to remember our wholeness and to dance with Life in all its beauty and complexity. It calls us to live from the heart, to embody Love not as a fleeting emotion but as our very essence. This is the tantric path to unity: finding the sacred in the sensual, the divine in the mundane, and the eternal in the moment.

In the same way that a single raindrop contains the reflection of the entire sky, "*Unio Mystica*" reminds us that we are both individual and universal, finite and infinite, human and divine. When we listen deeply, the song becomes an experience of timeless unity – an echo of the truth that there is, in the end, only Love. And in this Love, all polarities dissolve into the bliss of oneness.

The Inspiration

The inspiration to this song came from the following German poem of an unknown author:
Unio Mystica
Ich bin die Quelle und der große Strom,
Ich bin der Fels, der Steinmetz und der Dom;
Ich bin der Weg, der Wandrer und das Ziel,
Das Meer, das weiße Segel und der Kiel.
Ich bin Geburt und Tod und Sein und Nichts,
Des Rades Nabe und der Strahl des Lichts,
Des Himmels Körper und das Korn des Staubes,
Der Wind, das Welken und der Fall des Laubes,
Ich bin der Spieler und der Geigenton,
Ich bin das All, der Vater und der Sohn,
Der Keim in der Bewegung aller Dinge,
Das Kreisende in der Gestalt der Ringe,
Der Nu im Stellestehn der Ewigkeit,
Das weite ferne Jenseits aller Zeit,
Das große Du in Deiner dunklen Tiefe,
Das Handgelenk im Schreiben Deiner Briefe.
Ich bin das ich, das in Dir tiefer keimt,
Das Träumende, das in uns allen träumt,
Ich bin der jähe Schmerz in allem Leid,
Und die Befreiung, die vom Ich befreit.

The Lyrics

[Verse 1]
I am the source and the flowing stream,
I am the rock, the builder, and the dream.
I am the road, the traveler and the end,
The sea, the sail, and the keel that bends.
I am birth, death, and the being of none,
The hub of the wheel and the light of the sun.
I'm the sky above, and the dust below,
The wind, the withering, the falling leaf's glow.

[Chorus]
Unio Mystica, we are one,
In the circle of Life, it's all begun.
From the depths to the sky, we dance and play,
In the rhythm of Life, we find our way.
Unio Mystica, feel the flow,
Through the pain and joy, we rise and grow.

[Verse 2]
I'm the player, the music in the string,
I'm the universe, the father, and the king.
The seed that moves in all that's alive,
The circle spinning, where rings survive.
I am the now in eternity's grace,
The great beyond, the timeless space.
I'm the great "You" in your deepest dive,
The hand that moves when you write to survive.

[Chorus]
Unio Mystica, we are one,
In the circle of Life, it's all begun.
From the depths to the sky, we dance and play,
In the riddim of Life, we find our way.
Unio Mystica, feel the flow,
Through the pain and joy, we rise and grow.

[Bridge]
I'm the "I" that in you deeply grows,
The dreamer in us all that flows.
I am the pain in all that's cried,
And the freedom that from the self has died.

[Chorus]
Unio Mystica, we are one,
In the circle of Life, it's all begun.
From the depths to the sky, we dance and play,
In the riddim of Life, we find our way.
Unio Mystica, feel the flow,
Through the pain and joy, we rise and grow.

[Outro]
We are the circle, the dream and the light,
The players in the endless night.
Unio Mystica, we are all,
In the dance of Life, we rise and fall.

Om Mani Padme Hum
(Mantra Dub)

The mantra "*Om Mani Padme Hum*" is one of the most sacred and well-known mantras in Tibetan Buddhism. It is often called the "jewel in the lotus" mantra, symbolizing the transformation of ignorance into wisdom, and the unfolding of compassion and enlightenment. The six syllables of the mantra have deep meaning, each representing the purification of negative emotions and the embodiment of certain virtues:

- *Om*: Purifies pride and ego, representing the universal sound and the body of all Buddhas.
- *Ma*: Purifies jealousy and the feeling of possessiveness, embodying ethics and compassion.
- *Ni*: Purifies passion and desire, cultivating patience.
- *Pad*: Purifies ignorance and prejudice, fostering perseverance.
- *Me*: Purifies greed and possessiveness, encouraging concentration and mindfulness.
- *Hum*: Purifies hatred and aggression, leading to wisdom and unity.

The mantra encapsulates the essence of the Bodhisattva of Compassion, Avalokiteshvara, calling for inner Peace, Love for all beings, and the development of a compassionate heart.

Contemplation on "Om Mani Padme Hum"

As you chant the mantra, it serves as a meditation tool to align body, mind, and spirit with the qualities of compassion, purity, and enlightenment. The mantra invites you to reflect on the nature of suffering in the world and the transformative potential within you to turn negativity into positivity, ignorance into wisdom, and separation into unity. Like a lotus that grows in muddy waters but blossoms in pristine beauty, the mantra teaches that enlightenment is possible despite the challenges and struggles of Life.

"Om Mani Padme Hum" invites us to cultivate a compassionate heart, not just for ourselves, but for all sentient beings. It helps to dissolve the illusion of separateness, urging us to realize the interconnectedness of all Life.

Om Mani Padme Hum in the Context of the Essene Gospel of Love and Peace

In the context of the Essene Gospel of Love and Peace, the mantra *"Om Mani Padme Hum"* can be seen as a call to align with the sacred wisdom and compassion of the natural world. The Essenes emphasized purity of the body, mind, and spirit, a reverence for the elements, and deep communion with both the Heavenly Father and Mother Earth. Just as the mantra calls for the purification of negative emotions and the blossoming of spiritual insight, the teachings of the Essenes emphasize harmony with nature and the divine, calling for a return to simplicity, purity, and Love.

The Essene Gospel of Love and Peace speaks of the healing powers of nature and the angels of the elements, urging humanity to live in accordance with the laws of the Earth and the universe. Similarly, *"Om Mani Padme Hum"* can be seen as a spiritual practice that fosters a deep connection to the universal energies of compassion and wisdom. In both teachings, there is a recognition of the sacred unity of all Life, the power of purification, and the transformative journey toward enlightenment.

The mantra and the gospel together remind us that Peace, Love, and harmony with the Earth and each other are central to spiritual enlightenment. Whether through chanting "*Om Mani Padme Hum*" or following the natural, peaceful way of the Essenes, both paths encourage us to cultivate a compassionate, loving heart, and live in unity with the divine forces that sustain Life.

The Lyrics

Om Mani Padme Hum

Extra Single: Om Mani Padme Hum, Let the Love and Healing come

This song, published as a single and being a heartfelt rendition of the sacred mantra "*Om Mani Padme Hum*", carries a message of profound Love, healing, and transformation. It blends the ancient vibration of the mantra with the universal call for compassion, inviting listeners to open their hearts and allow the healing energies of Love to flow through them. The phrase "Let the Love and healing come" acts as both a prayer and a mantra in itself – an invocation for personal and collective awakening, reminding us that the power to heal lies within each of us.

Love and Healing through the Mantra

Om Mani Padme Hum is often called the mantra of compassion. In this song, it becomes a bridge between the sacred and the mundane, channelling the timeless energies of healing and wholeness into our present reality. Love and healing are not distant ideals but transformative forces available here and now. As we chant or listen, we begin to feel these forces dissolving barriers – within our hearts, between us and others, and even between us and nature.

The mantra's essence is a reminder that healing begins with compassion – first for ourselves, then for the world around us. It encourages us to embrace our own imperfections with tenderness and to extend that same loving kindness to all beings. Healing is not about escaping pain but about integrating and transforming it through Love, just as the lotus grows out of the mud and blossoms into purity.

Surrendering to the Flow of Love

The words "Let the Love and healing come" express a profound act of surrender. In a world where we often feel the need to control, protect, or guard ourselves, the song invites us to let go, to allow the natural flow of Love to wash over us. This surrender is not weakness; it is a return to our true nature – a state of openness, trust, and unity with the divine flow of Life.

Through the song, we are reminded that Love is the foundation of all healing. When we open ourselves to Love, we invite harmony into our being. This harmony restores balance – within the body, mind, and soul – and allows us to reconnect with the deeper truth that we are already whole. Healing is not about becoming someone new, but about remembering who we truly are.

A Collective Prayer for Peace

"*Om Mani Padme Hum*, Let the Love and Healing Come" also acts as a collective prayer, a call for Peace and unity in a world that is often fragmented by fear and division. As we chant or listen, we become part of a larger web of healing energy, joining with countless others who hold the same intention for Peace, Love, and compassion. The mantra, repeated by many across centuries, becomes a living force that transcends time and space – uniting hearts, across borders, in the shared desire for healing.

The song emphasizes that healing is not only personal but also collective. As each of us heals, we contribute to the healing of the whole. Just as a ripple in water spreads outward, our acts of compassion and Love affect the world in ways we may never fully see or understand. The song encourages us to become vessels of Love, allowing the healing energy to move through us and touch the lives of others.

A Pathway to Inner Peace

Ultimately, "*Om Mani Padme Hum*, Let the Love and Healing Come" offers a pathway to inner Peace. It reminds us that Peace is not something we have to search for outside ourselves; it is already within, waiting to be awakened. The mantra serves as a key to unlocking this Peace, dissolving the noise of the mind and guiding us back to the stillness of the heart.

In chanting or listening to this song, we are invited into a sacred space where Love reigns and healing flows freely. It teaches us that no matter what we face – suffering, confusion, or loss – the answer is always the same: Love. When we let the Love and healing come, we align ourselves with the eternal dance of compassion, grace, and unity, embodying the mantra's essence in every breath and every moment.

This song, then, is more than music – it is a prayer, a meditation, and a doorway to healing. Through its vibrations, it reminds us that Love is both the path and the destination, and that healing is always within reach, as soon as we allow it. With each repetition of *Om Mani Padme Hum*, we affirm our place in the flow of Life's infinite Love, calling forth the healing that the world – and our own hearts – so deeply need.

The Lyrics

[Verse 1]
Feel the rhythm of the Earth below,
Mountains high and rivers flow.
In every heart, a seed is sown,
To find the Peace, to call it home.
The lotus blooms beneath the sun,
We are all one, the journey's begun.
With every breath, I call Your name,
Om Mani Padme Hum, it's all the same.

[Chorus]
Om Mani Padme Hum,
Love's the way we overcome.
From the heart, we rise above,
Chanting Peace and sharing Love.
Om Mani Padme Hum, in the light, we are one.
Let the Love and healing come,
Om Mani Padme Hum.

[Verse 2]
Feel the spirit rising in the air,
In every soul, there's Love to share.
Through the struggle, through the pain,
We lift our voices, we rise again.
No more borders, no more fight,
Just the sound of Love in the night.
With every breath, the heart beats strong,
Om Mani Padme Hum, where we belong.

[Chorus]
Om Mani Padme Hum, Love's the way we overcome.
From the heart, we rise above,
Chanting Peace and sharing Love.
Om Mani Padme Hum, in the light, we are one.
Let the Love and healing come,
Om Mani Padme Hum.

[Bridge]
Feel the power in the words we say,
The world will change with Love today.
No more sorrow, no more hate,
Let's open up the golden gate.
The lotus blooms in every heart,
Om Mani Padme Hum, it's where we start.

[Chorus]
Om Mani Padme Hum, Love's the way we overcome.
From the heart, we rise above,
Chanting Peace and sharing Love.
Om Mani Padme Hum, in the light, we are one.
Let the Love and healing come,
Om Mani Padme Hum.

[Outro]
Om Mani Padme Hum, we are one under the sun.
Om Mani Padme Hum, let the Love and healing come.
Om Mani Padme Hum … Om Mani Padme Hum.
Om Mani Padme Hum

Feel the sunshine, let it in,
A brand new day for Peace to begin.
In every heart, there is a way,
To light the dark and heal today.
With every beat, the rhythm flows,
Om Mani Padme Hum, and the Love it grows.
We plant the seed and watch it bloom,
In Peace we walk, in Love we tune.

ooho ooho, ooho

Om Mani Padme Hum, …
Love's the way we overcome.
From the heart, we rise above,
Chanting Peace and sharing Love.
You're welcome here today.
With every beat, the rhythm flows,
Om Mani Padme Hum, and the Love it grows.
We plant the seed and watch it bloom,
In Peace we walk, in Love we tune.
Feel the sunshine, let it in,
A brand new day for Peace to begin.
In every heart, there is a way,
To light the dark and heal today.
With every beat, the rhythm flows,
Om Mani Padme Hum, and the Love it grows.
We plant the seed and watch it bloom,
In Peace we walk, in Love we tune.

ooho ooho, ooho

From the rivers to the mountain high,
We spread the Love beneath the sky.
Every moment, the message clear,
Om Mani Padme Hum, the world can hear.
No division, no more fear,
Just the sound of Love drawing near.
With every chant, we break the chain,
Om Mani Padme Hum, we rise again.
we rise again.
Feel the sunshine, let it in,
A brand new day for Peace to begin.
In every heart, there is a way,
To light the dark and heal today.
No division, no more fear,
Just the sound of Love drawing near.
With every chant, we break the chain,
Om Mani Padme Hum, we rise again.

Walking With The Great Spirit

"Walking with the Great Spirit" is a journey into the sacred essence of Life. The song, which is inspired by the Native American's concept of the Great Spirit, reflects a connection with something vast, timeless, and divine – the force that pervades all of existence. It is an invitation to walk consciously through the world, guided by a deep reverence for Life, aware that every step is sacred, every breath is a gift, and every encounter holds meaning.

To walk with the Great Spirit is to move through Life in harmony, aligned with the rhythms of nature and the wisdom of the heart. It is not a physical journey, but a spiritual practice – a way of being in the world that acknowledges the divine presence in all things. The song encourages us to recognize that we are never alone; the Great Spirit walks with us in every moment, in the silence of the forest, in the whisper of the wind, and in the song of the birds.

A Path of Reverence and Humility

The act of walking with the Great Spirit is also a practice of humility. It reminds us to tread lightly upon the Earth, treating all beings with kindness and respect. Every step becomes a prayer of gratitude, every interaction a chance to express Love. In this walk, there is no rush, no need to arrive anywhere – only the unfolding of the present moment, filled with awe and wonder.

The song speaks to the importance of slowing down and becoming aware. It invites us to let go of distractions and worries, to quiet the mind, and to listen deeply to the voice of the Spirit that speaks through the natural world and through our own hearts. When we walk with the Great Spirit, we learn to trust the path, even when it takes unexpected turns.

Embracing the Journey

"Walking with the Great Spirit" teaches us that Life is not about reaching a destination, but about embracing the journey itself. Each step is part of a larger dance, a continuous flow of experiences that shape and transform us. The journey with the Spirit is one of openness – open eyes to see beauty, open ears to hear truth, and an open heart to receive Love.

This song reminds us that the Spirit is found not only in the grand moments but also in the small, seemingly insignificant ones: in a smile, in the rustling of leaves, or in the stillness of a sunrise. Walking with the Spirit means honouring these moments and recognizing the sacred in the everyday.

The Great Spirit as Guide and Companion

The song reflects the idea that the Great Spirit is both guide and companion on this journey. When we walk with the Spirit, we are never lost, even in times of darkness or uncertainty. The Spirit whispers encouragement when the road feels hard, offering comfort in moments of doubt. Walking with the Great Spirit means knowing that we are held by something greater than ourselves, a presence that leads us gently toward wisdom, Peace, and fulfilment.

Ultimately, "Walking with the Great Spirit" is a song about unity – unity with nature, with others, and with the divine. It reminds us that we belong to the Earth, to each other, and to the Great Spirit that connects all Life. When we walk with this awareness, our steps become part of the sacred rhythm of the universe, and we realize that every journey is holy, every path blessed.

Through this song, we are invited to embody Love, Peace, and gratitude as we walk – knowing that with every step, we are in communion with the Great Spirit, carrying its presence in our hearts and spreading its light wherever the journey leads.

The Lyrics

[Intro]
(Ho, hey, ho… ho, hey, ho…)
We call to the sky, we call to the earth,
We call to the fire, we call to the water.
(Ho, hey, ho… ho, hey, ho…)
Great Spirit, hear our song,
Guide us as we walk along.

[Verse 1]
Great Spirit, in the wind that blows,
In the river's flow, where the wild grass grows.
You are the sun, you are the rain,
You are the Life in the earth's great vein.

From the mountains high to the valleys deep,
In the silence of night, where the spirits sleep,
We feel your power, we feel your grace,
We see your light in every face.

[Chorus]
Oh, Great Spirit, in the sky,
Guide our hearts, teach us to fly.
Oh, Great Spirit, in the land,
Hold us in your sacred hand.
(Ho, hey, ho… ho, hey, ho…)
(Ho, hey, ho… ho, hey, ho…)

[instrumental interlude]

[Verse 2]
You are the eagle, soaring free,
The ancient wisdom in every tree.
You are the drumbeat in our chest,
The voice that calls us to do our best.

With every step we take, we know,
The Great Spirit's in the wind that blows.
We honor the ground, the sky so wide,
For you are the truth that lives inside.

[Chorus]
Oh, Great Spirit, in the sky,
Guide our hearts, teach us to fly.
Oh, Great Spirit, in the land,
Hold us in your sacred hand.
(Ho, hey, ho… ho, hey, ho…)
(Ho, hey, ho… ho, hey, ho…)

[instrumental interlude]

[Chorus]
Oh, Great Spirit, in the sky,
Guide our hearts, teach us to fly.
Oh, Great Spirit, in the land,
Hold us in your sacred hand.
(Ho, hey, ho… ho, hey, ho…)
(Ho, hey, ho… ho, hey, ho…)

[Bridge]
In the flames that rise, in the water's flow,
In the seeds we plant, in the Love we sow.
Great Spirit, we are one,
Underneath the same great sun.

Let us walk the sacred way,
With every breath, with every day.
We sing your name, we feel your light,
Guide us through the endless night.

[Chorus]
Oh, Great Spirit, in the sky,
Guide our hearts, teach us to fly.
Oh, Great Spirit, in the land,
Hold us in your sacred hand.
(Ho, hey, ho… ho, hey, ho…)
(Ho, hey, ho… ho, hey, ho…)

[Outro]
(Ho, hey, ho… ho, hey, ho…)
We call to the sky, we call to the earth,
We call to the fire, we call to the water.

(Ho, hey, ho… ho, hey, ho…)
Great Spirit, hear our song,
Guide us as we walk along.

[Chorus]
Oh, Great Spirit, in the sky,
Guide our hearts, teach us to fly.
Oh, Great Spirit, in the land,
Hold us in your sacred hand.
(Ho, hey, ho… ho, hey, ho…)
(Ho, hey, ho… ho, hey, ho…)

[Outro]
(Ho, hey, ho… ho, hey, ho…)
We call to the sky, we call to the earth,
We call to the fire, we call to the water.
(Ho, hey, ho… ho, hey, ho…)
Great Spirit, hear our song,
Guide us as we walk along.

Appendix

Further Reading

Peace - Real Power Comes from Love, not Hate

A Book About Pacifism, Non-Violence and Civil Disobedience

Jay B Joyful, Jörg Berchem

Gesellschaft, Politik & Medien
Paperback
372 Seiten
ISBN-13: 9783758317477
Verlag: Books on Demand
Erscheinungsdatum: 18.12.2023
Sprache: Englisch
Schlagworte: Frieden, Pazifismus, Gewaltfreiheit, ziviler Ungehorsam, Gewaltlosigkeit

☆ ☆ ☆ ☆ ☆ 0 Bewertungen

erhältlich als:

BUCH 16,99 €   E-BOOK 9,99 €

Order from any bookshop, or https://Peace.Joyful-Life.org

Also available in German.

The Gospel of Love and Peace

Essene Books I - IV

Jörg Berchem (Hrsg.)

Spiritualität & Esoterik
Hardcover
420 Seiten
ISBN-13: 9783739241692
Verlag: BoD - Books on Demand
Erscheinungsdatum: 31.08.2016
Sprache: Englisch
Schlagworte: Essener, Qumran, Gospel, Essenes, Friedensevangelium

★ ★ ★ ★ ★

erhältlich als:

BUCH 29,00 €   E-BOOK 16,99 €

Order from any bookshop, or https://GLP.Joyful-Life.org

Also available in German.

The Sevenfold Peace

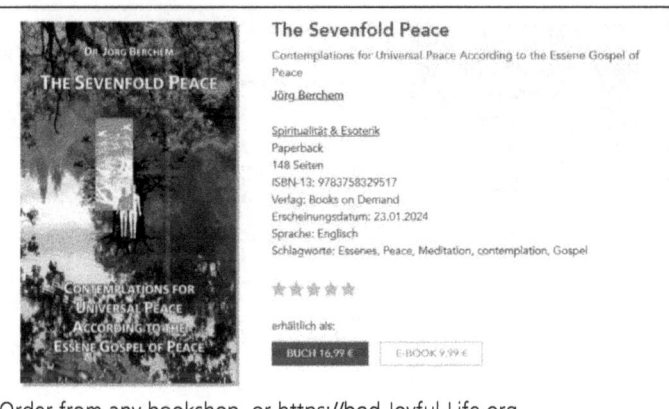

Contemplations for Universal Peace According to the Essene Gospel of Peace

Jörg Berchem

Spiritualität & Esoterik
Paperback
148 Seiten
ISBN-13: 9783758329517
Verlag: Books on Demand
Erscheinungsdatum: 23.01.2024
Sprache: Englisch
Schlagworte: Essenes, Peace, Meditation, contemplation, Gospel

★ ★ ★ ★ ★

erhältlich als:

BUCH 16,99 €   E-BOOK 9,99 €

Order from any bookshop, or https://bod.Joyful-Life.org

Also available in German.

Meditations of the Children of Light

Communions with the Angels according to the Essene Gospel of Peace

Jörg Berchem

Spiritualität & Esoterik
Paperback
148 Seiten
ISBN-13: 9783758326561
Verlag: Books on Demand
Erscheinungsdatum: 10.01.2024
Sprache: Englisch
Schlagworte: Essener, Székely, Angels, Meditation, Engel

★ ★ ★ ★ ★

erhältlich als:

BUCH 18,99 €   E-BOOK 9,99 €

Order from any bookshop, or https://bod.Joyful-Life.org

Also available in German.

The Teachings of the Essenes

From Enoch to the Dead Sea Scrolls

Edmond Bordeaux Székely, Dr. Jörg Berchem (Hrsg.)

Gesellschaft, Politik & Medien
Paperback
148 Seiten
ISBN-13: 9783758300127
Verlag: Books on Demand
Erscheinungsdatum: 01.11.2023
Sprache: Englisch
Schlagworte: Essenes, Essener, Qumran, Jésus, Gospel

★ ★ ★ ★ ★ 0 Bewertungen

erhältlich als:

BUCH 16,00 €   E-BOOK 5,99 €

Order from any bookshop, or https://bod.Joyful-Life.org

Also available in German.

Double Album with 24 songs

Available on all well-known streaming platforms.

www.Joyful-Life.org